# Learn to Draw Manga

# MANGA
## DRAGONS

Illustrated by
Richard Jones & Jorge Santillan

**PowerKiDS**
press™
**New York**

Published in 2013 by The Rosen Publishing Group, Inc.
29 East 21st Street, New York, NY 10010

First Edition

Produced for Rosen by Calcium Creative Ltd
Editor: Sarah Eason
Editor for Rosen: Sara Antill
Book Design: Paul Myerscough

Illustrations by Richard Jones and Jorge Santillan


Library of Congress Cataloging-in-Publication Data

Jones, Richard, 1979–
 Manga dragons / by Richard Jones & Jorge Santillan. — 1st ed.
    p. cm. — (Learn to draw manga)
 Includes index.
 ISBN 978-1-4488-7874-1 (library binding) —
ISBN 978-1-4488-7945-8 (pbk.) — ISBN 978-1-4488-7951-9 (6-pack)
1.  Dragons in art—Juvenile literature. 2.  Comic books, strips, etc.—
Japan—Technique—Juvenile literature. 3.  Cartooning—Technique
—Juvenile literature.  I. Santillan, Jorge. II. Title.
NC1764.5.D72J36 2013
743'.87—dc23

                                2011052909

Manufactured in the United States of America

CPSIA Compliance Information: Batch #B4S12PK: For Further Information contact Rosen Publishing, New York, New York at 1-800-237-9932

# Contents

# Drawing Manga Dragons

"Manga" is a Japanese word that means "comic." You can use this inspiring illustration style to draw almost anything, including dragons!

## Manga dragon world

In this book, we are going to show you how to draw some spectacular, awe-inspiring dragons, Manga-style!

# You will need

To create your Manga dragons, you will need some equipment:

## Sketchpad or paper

Try to use good quality paper from an art store.

## Pencils

A set of good drawing pencils are key to creating great dragon drawings.

## Eraser

Use this to remove any unwanted lines.

## Paintbrush, paints, and pens

The final stage for all your drawings will be to add color. We have used paints to complete the Manga dragons in this book. If you prefer, you could use pens.

# Leaping Dragon

Wings open and snorting smoke, this young dragon is ready to attack!

## Step 1

Draw the outline for your dragon and give him a leaping pose.

## Step 2

Add detailed lines for the head, tail, and wings. Pencil further detail on the face.

## Step 3

Add some light shading to the body, face, and claws. Add the long whiskers on the jaw.

## Step 4

Color your dragon a rich orange. Use a soft green for the belly, and give him bright, green eyes. Color the wing skin cream.

# Fiery Dragon

Fairy-tales are full of stories about fire-breathing dragons that could burn a village with one breath! Create your own flame-breathing monster.

## Step 1

Use a long, circular shape for the body. Draw cone shapes for the legs and arms. Take time to draw the curving neck and the spiked head. Add the feet and claws.

## Step 2

Add some detail with a row of spikes along the neck and end of the tail. Pencil the flames.

## Step 3

Draw lines across the chest and belly, and a ragged edge to the wings. Pencil feathers on the legs and add some shading to the mouth.

## Step 4

Erase any unwanted, rough lines. Add some spots to the body and neck.

## Sharpen your skills

Try a different pose in which your dragon's head is upright.

# Step 5

A beautiful orange red completes this fiery monster. Color the back, legs, head, and wing sections in this shade. Use a pale brown-pink color for the belly and wing skin, and yellow for the fire!

# Baby Dragon

Adult dragons may be terrifying, but babies are utterly cute!

## Step 1

Draw a circle for the belly and head. Pencil the tail, arms, legs, feet, and beak. Add the horns and claws.

## Step 2

Add the scales on the baby's neck, back, and tail. Draw the horns on its cheeks and nose. Pencil the eyes.

## Step 3

Add shading to the eyes to give them expression. Add shadow under the dragon. Erase any unwanted lines.

## Step 4

Paint this baby a brilliant, bright blue. Use a beige-brown color for the body and feet pads. Pink is perfect for the tongue and red eyes pop out against the blue face. Add some highlights to the nose, head, and tail with white paint.

# Water Dragon

Some dragons live in caves, others are water-dwelling beasts that lunge at passing boats!

## Step 1

This water monster is clinging to a rock. Draw a triangle shape for the rock outline. Use a long, oval shape for the body, a circle for the head, and a curved, sweeping crescent for the tail. Pencil the arms, legs, and claws.

## Step 2

Add detail by drawing the eyes, nostrils, and tongue.

## Step 3

Draw a long, spiked ridge to the dragon's neck and back. Pencil the end of the tail. Add the horns on the head and nose.

## Step 4

Use a very fine-tipped pencil to add the teeth and pattern lines on the body.

## Sharpen your skills

If you'd prefer to have your dragon sitting on the rock, try this pose instead.

# Step 5

Use a strong, rich yellow for the chest, neck and back frills, and the wing skin. Use this color on the tip of the tail, too. Choose a rich blue and green palette for the face, neck, back, and tail, too. Add a wash of deep blue for the water beneath.

# Lovable Dragon

When this smoke-breathing dragon grows up, he'll be awesome. For now, keep him cute!

## Step 1

Draw two overlapping egg shapes for the body and rear. Use another oval for the head. Pencil triangles for the ear, wing, and tail tip.

## Step 2

Add the eyes, horns on the head, and mouth. Pencil the claws and scales on the back. Add the edges of the ear.

## Step 3

Use a fine-tipped pencil to add a dotted pattern to the legs, marks on the belly, and shading.

## Step 4

Color your cute dragon with a deep red and a bright yellow. Use brown for the claws and extra shading. Add white highlights.

# Two-Headed Dragon

This is a dragon to be feared.
It has not one, but two heads
with deadly, snapping jaws!

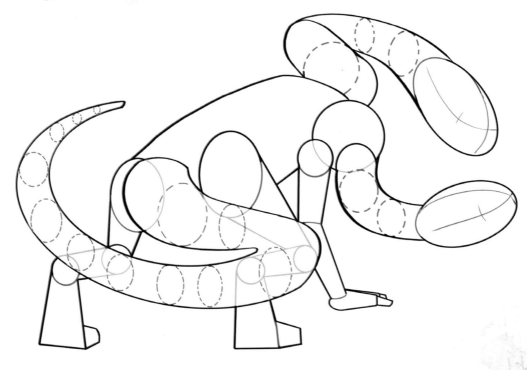

## Step 1

Draw the body, legs, and tail.
Pencil the claws. Then add
the two curving necks and
circles for the heads.

## Step 2

Pencil the wings, and add some finer lines to the tail and heads.

## Step 3

Add scales to the neck and tail. Pencil horns on the heads. Then draw the eyes.

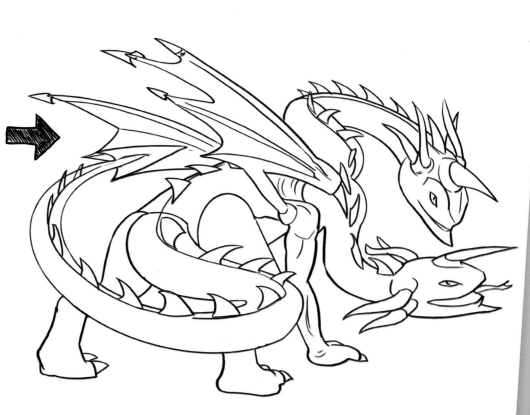

## Step 4

Erase any rough lines and add shading and the marks on the tail.

## Sharpen your skills

How about a three-headed dragon? Why not try a head with curved teeth?

# Step 5

Deep blue-gray and bright purples are perfect for the legs, neck, wings, and tail of this monstrous beast. Use a pink for one head and add flashes of it to the rest of the wing and rear legs. Use cream for the dragon's horns and wing tips and a brown for its underbelly and the underside of the tail.

# Flying Dragon

This dragon is sweeping
through the skies and casting
a shadow across the land.

## Step 1

Draw the head and pencil the body behind.
Add arms, legs, and the small circles for
the shoulders. Draw a long line from each
shoulder, then pencil another smaller
circle and three lines for the wings.

## Step 2

Draw the long wing arms
and pencil the dragon's beak.

## Step 3

Add finer details to the head,
including the horns, and the
claws and tail tip.

# Step 4

Draw in the wing skin and the detail of the head and body. Add shading to the head, body, and wing arms.

## Sharpen your skills

You can change the angle and style of the head, as shown here.

## Step 5

This evil-looking monster has a dark green body. Add touches of light green for areas, such as the legs, arm wings, head, and tail. Use cream and orange for the wing skin. Give the beast a dark red mouth and wicked yellow eyes!

# More Dragons

If you've loved drawing Manga dragons, try some more!

## Dragon King

Try out this all-powerful beast.

## Perching Dragon

This dragon is perching on a cliff top, ready to pounce!

# Two-Tailed Dragon

Some dragons
have two heads,
others have
double tails!

# Ancient Dragon

This beast has woken from
a 1,000-year sleep, and he is
really mad!

# Glossary

**character** (KER-ik-tur) A fictional, or made-up person. Can also mean the features that you recognize something or someone by.

**deadly** (DED-lee) Can kill.

**detail** (dih-TAYL) The smaller, finer lines that are used to add important features to a character drawing, such as eyes, ears, and hair.

**dwelling** (DWEL-ing) Living.

**erase** (ih-RAYS) To remove.

**expression** (ik-SPREH-shun) A look on someone's face that can tell you what they are thinking.

**fine-tipped** (fyn-TIHPD) A sharp tip of a pencil or pen.

**highlights** (HY-lytz) Light parts.

**lunge** (LUNJ) Moving suddenly forward.

**nostrils** (NOS-trulz) Openings on a person or animal's head through which they breathe air.

**outline** (OWT-lyn) A very simple line that provides the shape for a drawing.

**overlapping** (oh-ver-LAP-ing) Crossing over.

**palette** (PA-lit) A range of colors.

**pose** (POHZ) The way something or somebody stands.

**ragged** (RA-ged) Having a rough edge.

**scales** (SKAYLZ) Small, hard shapes that overlap to create a reptile or fish's skin.

**shading** (SHAYD-ing) Creating lots of soft, heavy lines to add shadow and depth to a drawing.

**snorting** (SNORT-ing) Pushing something, such as smoke, out of the nostrils.

**underbelly** (UN-der-beh-lee) The soft stomach area.

# Further Reading

Amberlyn, J. C. *Drawing Manga Animals, Chibis and Other Adorable Creatures.* New York: Watson-Guptill, 2009.

Bergin, Mark. *How to Draw Dragons.* How to Draw. New York: PowerKids Press, 2011.

Giannotta, Andrés Bernardo. *How to Draw Manga.* Mineola, NY: Dover Publications, 2010.

Staple, Sandra. *Drawing Dragons: Learn How to Create Fantastic Fire-Breathing Dragons.* Berkeley, CA: Ulysses Press, 2008.

Welch, Laura, and Bodie Hodge. *Dragons: Legends and Lore of Dinosaurs.* Green Forest, AR: Master Books, 2011.

# Websites

Due to the changing nature of Internet links, PowerKids Press has developed an online list of websites related to the subject of this book. This site is updated regularly. Please use this link to access the list: www.powerkidslinks.com/ltdm/dragon/

# Index

**A**

adding details, 6, 9, 12, 15–16, 18–19, 21–22, 25–26

adding highlights, 13, 19

ancient dragons, 28

**B**

baby dragons, 12–13

**C**

colors, 7, 11, 13, 17, 19, 23, 27

**E**

erasing, 5, 10, 13, 22

**F**

fire-breathing dragons, 6–7, 8–11, 18–19

flying dragons, 24–27

**L**

leaping dragons, 6–7

**M**

more dragon characters, 28–29

**O**

outlines, 6, 8, 12, 14, 18, 20, 24

**P**

painting, 7, 11, 13, 17, 19, 23, 27

poses, 6, 10, 16

**S**

shading, 7, 9, 11, 13, 19, 22, 26

shapes, 8, 14, 18, 20, 24

**T**

two-headed dragons, 20–23

two-tailed dragons, 28

**W**

water-dwelling dragons, 14–17

**Y**

young dragons, 6–7, 18–19